# Wow! Animals

## A Book of Extraordinary Facts

KINGFISHER

# Bird-watching

Let's say hello to the largest and the smallest birds in the world.

Hi, I'm an ostrich, how do you do? Did you hatch from an egg like me?

## I spy

The ostrich has the largest eyes of any animal on land, which helps this bird to keep a look out for lions and other hungry predators.

With its huge fluffy feathers, the ostrich is the biggest bird of all. An ostrich can't fly, but this bird is super speedy and it can outrun most animals.

only Mr Cheetah runs faster than me!

4

The female ostrich lays huge eggs. One of her eggs weighs the same as 24 chicken eggs. If you'd like one for breakfast, it will take 90 minutes to cook!

Look at me! I'm a **ruby-throated hummingbird.**
I'm a boy — you can tell from my colours.

## Yum, yum

This hummingbird is tiny but he eats a LOT. He likes tasty spiders and flies, but loves sweet nectar from flowers most of all. It gives him the energy he needs to fly so fast!

Do you know why a hummingbird hums? Its wings beat so fast that it makes a humming sound. These incredible birds can fly backwards, too!

I'm a **bee hummingbird** and I'm the smallest bird in the world. I'm only **5** centimetres long.

**Uh-oh!** This doesn't have feathers!

## Whose tail is it?

# Big teeth

What makes crocodiles and lions so scary?
Perhaps it's all those big teeth!

I'm a crocodile.

Watch out for my tail!

## Big smile

When a crocodile loses a tooth, another one grows in its place. A crocodile may grow as many as 3000 teeth in its lifetime. Yikes!

A crocodile stores fat in its powerful tail. If a crocodile can't find anything to eat, it lives on the fat and can last nearly two years between meals!

I have **60** to **70** teeth.

People only have **32**.

Ha ha!

Crocodiles are reptiles, which means their blood is cold, not warm like yours. A croc lies in the sunshine to warm up, and when it's too hot, it opens its mouth to cool down!

I am a male Lion. You can call me Mr Lion.

Roarrrrr

Baby lion cubs purr like pussycats. But by the time they have their first birthday, they have learned to roar! Then you can hear them 8 kilometres away!

whose bottom is this?

## Wow!

A male lion is the only cat with a handsome mane. A mane helps him to attract a girlfriend, a female lion, called a lioness.

When a lion is hungry, it opens its jaws very wide indeed. A lion has an enormous bite, which helps it to tear up food.

7

# Gentle giants

These plant-loving animals might seem big and scary, but they are gentle creatures really.

We're elephants and we're very nosy!

## Wow!
Elephants are the largest animals living on land and their tusks are the biggest teeth of any land animal, too.

I'm a gorilla! I like to walk, just like you.

To help stay cool, an elephant uses its trunk to squirt muddy water all over its body. When the mud dries, it hardens and protects the elephant's skin from the sun.

8

# I'm a blue whale.

The blue whale swims in all the oceans on the planet. It needs a lot of room because it's the biggest animal that has ever lived!

*Where are you off to, little fish?*

*I weigh as much as 30 elephants!*

The Eastern Lowland gorilla in Africa is the biggest ape of all. This gorilla is a friendly, peace-loving animal that lives in large families, a bit like you!

Whales sing to each other underwater. Their songs can travel for incredible distances – sometimes from one side of an ocean to the other.

9

# Deep blue sea

The sea is full of amazing creatures, big and small.
Let's say hello to two mighty meat-eaters.

I'm a **tiger shark,**
nice to **eat** you.

I mean, **meet** you!

## I spy

A shark has an extra eyelid, which it closes to protect its eyes when fighting other sharks.

up ... up ...

Watch out! A shark will eat anything, from turtles and birds to fish and smaller sharks. It will even gobble up an old car tyre or oil can, it's not fussy.

... and away! I'm a **flying fish.**

Flying fish swim in the sea, but when they are chased by big, hungry fish they leap out of the water and glide though the air to escape.

I'm a **Sperm whale** and I am very, very clever.

Sperm whales have the biggest brain in the world. Their brain is 13 times bigger than a human man's brain.

## Wow!

A whale is a mammal, which means it breathes air. A sperm whale holds its breath for up to 90 minutes when it dives.

Hi, suckers!

A sperm whale will dive down two kilometres to the deepest parts of the ocean to find octopus, or its favourite meal – giant, squiggly squid!

# Something fishy

There's a magical world full of squiggly, wiggly creatures living at the bottom of the sea.

I'm an **OCTOPUS.**

Let's shake arms - I have **eight!**

## Wow!

The giant Pacific octopus has more than 2000 suckers on each arm! The suckers help the octopus to move along, or to grab a bite to eat!

Sea anemones look like pretty plants but they are animals with poisonous tentacles that sting passing fish.

A jellyfish isn't a jelly, or a fish. It's a sea creature without a heart, eyes or even a brain! But it does have a nasty sting. OUCH!

I'm a wibbly, wobbly jellyfish!

Hey, starfish! Where are you going?

Clownfish are the only fish that are not stung by anemones. They hide among the tentacles, so they won't be eaten by bigger fish.

Hello, clownfish!

Starfish aren't stars, or fish either! These sea creatures do have a mouth, though, and they eat oysters and little fish!

13

# Snap happy

Marching along the sea-bed, lobsters wear their skeletons like armour — on the outside!

Watch out, I'm a nippy **Lobster**.

## Quick march

Lobsters live on the seabed. They have ten legs — eight legs do the walking and two big claws are for catching and ripping up food.

Have you ever seen a blue, yellow or white American lobster? You are lucky if you have — they are very rare.

I'm a **blue** lobster.

14

If a lobster loses a leg or claw, perhaps in a fight, it grows another one – handy!

I'm a **yellow** lobster.

Lobsters taste food with their legs!

Snippety snip

I'm a **white** lobster.

# Wow!

Imagine if you never stopped growing! Well, a lobster grows its whole life. It can live to be 45 or 50 years old. Some may even live to be 100!

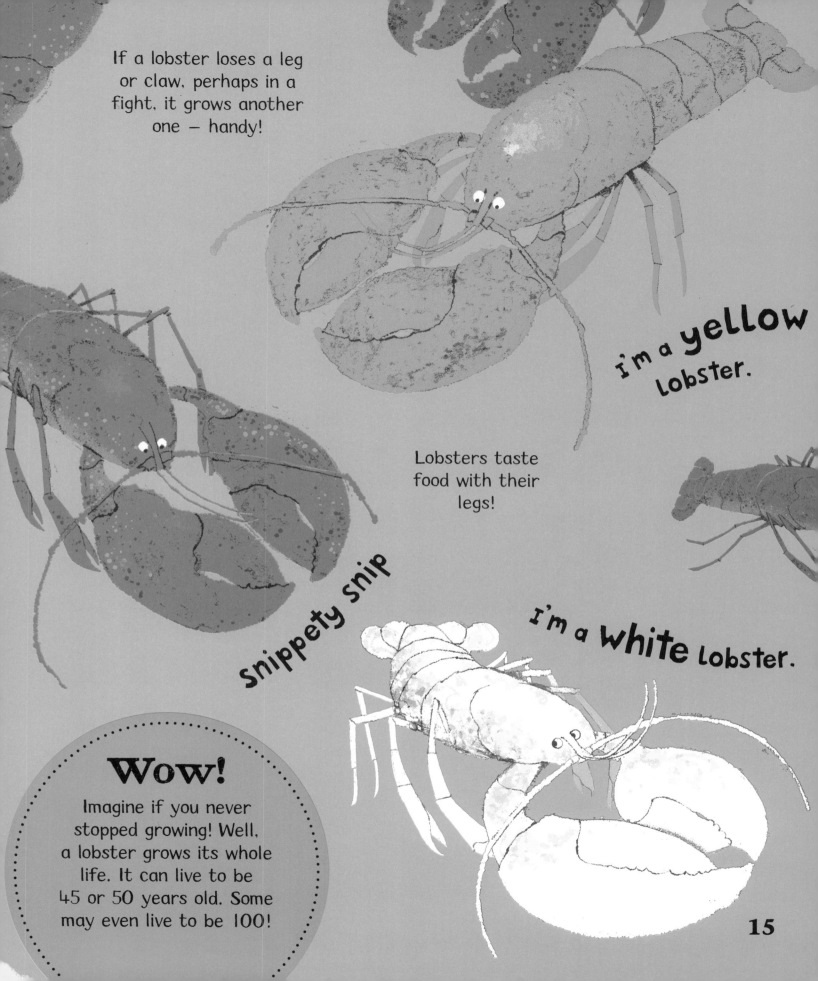

15

# Cool creatures

It's freezing cold at the North and South Poles, but there are some animals that like it that way!

## Ice to see you, I'm a polar bear.

### I live at the North Pole.

Polar bears are born on land, but they live most of their life on sea ice that floats on top of the Arctic Ocean.

## Doggy paddle

A polar bear is a great swimmer. It can swim in the freezing sea for up to 10 days if it wants to reach land or ice.

Polar bears are the biggest meat-eaters on land. Their favourite food is seals. GULP!

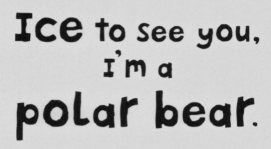

It's too cold for me here!

# Wow!

Penguins are flightless birds, which means they can't fly. But they are fantastic swimmers. Their wings act like flippers in the water.

There are lots of different kinds of penguins living in Antarctica, at the South Pole. Emperor penguins are the biggest and they are the only birds that lay their eggs on ice.

we're **penguins** - we live at the South Pole.

It's **fffffreezing** here!

A female emperor penguin lays one egg and then leaves to go hunting for four months! The male penguin balances the egg on his feet to keep the egg off the ice and stop it freezing. The penguin stays like that until the mummy comes back with food!

# Feathery friends

Birds are amazing creatures and they can do extraordinary things!

...albatross incoming!

## Wow!

The albatross is one of the biggest birds in the world. If you measure it from the tip of one wing to the tip of the other, it's almost as long as a car!

The wandering albatross is a champion flier! It soars high in the skies around the South Pole and will fly 1000 kilometres just to catch breakfast!

## I spy

Owls have huge eyes but they can't move them at all. An owl must swivel its whole head to look in a different direction.

Hellooooooooo!

When flamingos are born, their feathers are grey. As they grow, they eat tiny shrimp and plants that contain a red colour – the colour makes their feathers turn pink!

A flamingo eats with its head upside down. It wades into the water, catches food in its beak, then all the water runs out

whooosh

¡Hello!

I'm a flamingo. I eat upside down!

## Peckish

When a woodpecker is hungry, he goes a-pecking! With his strong beak, he can peck a tree 100 times a minute. The pecking makes the sticky grubs and insects come out!

Knock, knock. Who's there? A woodpecker!

19

# Super speedy!

Being fast on your feet, or on the wing, will help you catch food, escape danger or defend your babies.

whoosh

The peregrine falcon is the fastest animal on the planet. It likes to hunt in the air and can swoop at up to 180 kilometres per hour to catch smaller birds for tea!

## Wow!

A hippo spends most of its life lolling around in muddy pools, but if you tease it or get in its way, it will charge at you as fast as a horse!

Yikes!

Dragonflies are the fastest fliers of all the insects. A big dragonfly can zip along at 60 kilometres per hour. Dragonflies can fly in all directions too: up, down, backwards, forwards and side to side!

**No time to talk, I've got lunch to catch!**

Cheetahs are big cats. They are the fastest animal on four legs, which helps when what you eat is fast too!

A cheetah runs in short bursts to catch zippy gazelles and antelopes.

**I'm a hippopotamus, can you say that?**

A mummy hippo will run at another animal, or even a person, to scare them away or to protect her babies.

Slip, slither away ...

21

# Creep, slither, hop

Not all creatures are super sprinters. Let's meet a few that take things more slowly.

The golden orb-weaver spider spins a sticky web to trap beetles and flies. Then she creeps along her web, bites her prey, wraps them in spider silk and eats them later!

Welcome to my web!

## Wow!

These webs are so sticky that fishermen in the seas of the South Pacific use them to catch fish.

I'm a SSSSsnake.

A snake slithers along trees, and can sidewind along the ground, using its smooth belly scales.

Chameleons creep along branches very slowly, moving one leg at a time. They rock back and forth, mimicking leaves blowing in the wind.

When a chameleon is cold, it turns a dark colour, and when it's hot, it turns a light colour. And sometimes a chameleon changes colour just because it feels like it!

i'm a chameleon.

How rude!

Hoppity hop, I'm off!

Tasssssty!

A snake smells things using its tongue! That's why it flicks its tongue in and out.

Frogs have powerful back legs, which are very useful when they want to escape from a predator! They can hop up to ten times their body length. Can you?

23

# Creepy-crawlies!

Insects come in all shapes and sizes.
They may be tiny but they do incredible things.

oi!

we are monarch butterflies.

Monarch butterflies are champion fliers!

## Wow!

A grasshopper can jump about 20 times the length of its body. That's the same as you leaping across a football pitch.

Army ants go left, right!

Army ants are busy, busy insects! They don't have time to build nests because they're always on the march. At night, they form a ball around the queen ant, to protect her and her eggs. Then in the morning, they march on!

Monarchs will flutter thousands of kilometres in search of food, even crossing the Atlantic Ocean all the way from North America to Europe.

Flitter Flutter

Aren't we pretty?

# Yuck!

Some swallowtail butterfly caterpillars look like bird poo. This clever disguise means that most birds don't want to eat them. Would you?

# Honey bugs

Tiny bugs called aphids suck juice from plants and make a liquid called honeydew. Ants love it, so they tickle the aphids to make them give it up.

I'm a farmer ant.

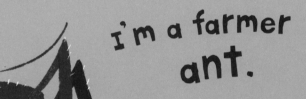
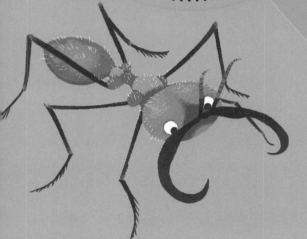

# Record-breakers

It isn't just insects that do amazing things. These record-breakers are of the four-legged kind!

Flutter

I'm a giraffe, I live in **Africa**.

I'm a **tiger**, I live in **Asia**.

## Wow!
With its long neck and legs, the giraffe is the tallest animal on the Earth! It has the same number of neck bones as you - but the giraffe's are longer.

Giraffes can moo, hiss and even whistle!

Tigers are the biggest cats in the cat family. Most tigers are orange with blackish brown stripes. The stripes help them hide in the jungle or woods.

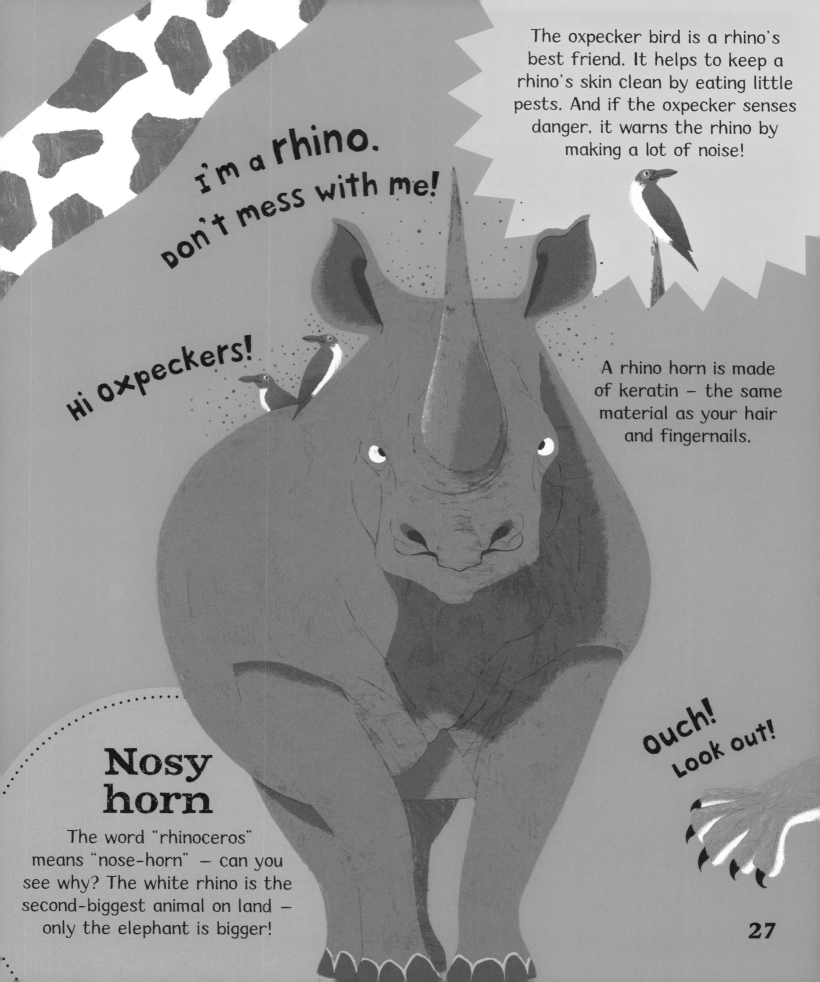

The oxpecker bird is a rhino's best friend. It helps to keep a rhino's skin clean by eating little pests. And if the oxpecker senses danger, it warns the rhino by making a lot of noise!

I'm a rhino. Don't mess with me!

Hi oxpeckers!

A rhino horn is made of keratin – the same material as your hair and fingernails.

Ouch! Look out!

# Nosy horn

The word "rhinoceros" means "nose-horn" – can you see why? The white rhino is the second-biggest animal on land – only the elephant is bigger!

# Above and below

Most animals spend their lives above the ground, but some prefer to burrow underground.

G'day, I'm a **kangaroo!**

Kangaroos and koala bears are marsupials that live in Australia. When a marsupial baby is born, it crawls into a pouch in its mummy's tummy!

**BOING**

A kangaroo is the only large animal that gets around by hopping!

I'm a mummy **koala bear**

and **I'm a joey!**

Koalas aren't bears, even though they look like cute teddy bears! They spend most of their life sleeping and eating eucalyptus leaves.

## Wow!
Baby kangaroos and koalas are called joeys. When they're born, they're only the size of a tiny bean!

## I spy

Moles can't see at all but that doesn't matter because they spend their time underground, digging long tunnels, sniffing out worms, insects and other tasty treats!

Prairie dogs are a bit like squirrels. They love company so they live together in a huge network of underground burrows. They see very well and keep watch on their enemies from kilometres away!

We're **prairie dogs!**

I am a **mole** and I live in a hole!

## True love

Prairie dogs spend a lot of time looking after each other. They clean each other's fur and then they kiss!

Who's there?  29

# Best friends

Human beings have always lived with animals around them — most of them we like, but not all!

Girl goats are called nannies and boys are called billys. There are more than 300 kinds of goat, and they all have a beard on their chin, even the girls!

## I spy

If you look closely, you'll see that goats have rectangular-shaped pupils in their eyes (and so do hippos!).

I'm a baby goat

I'm called a *kid!*

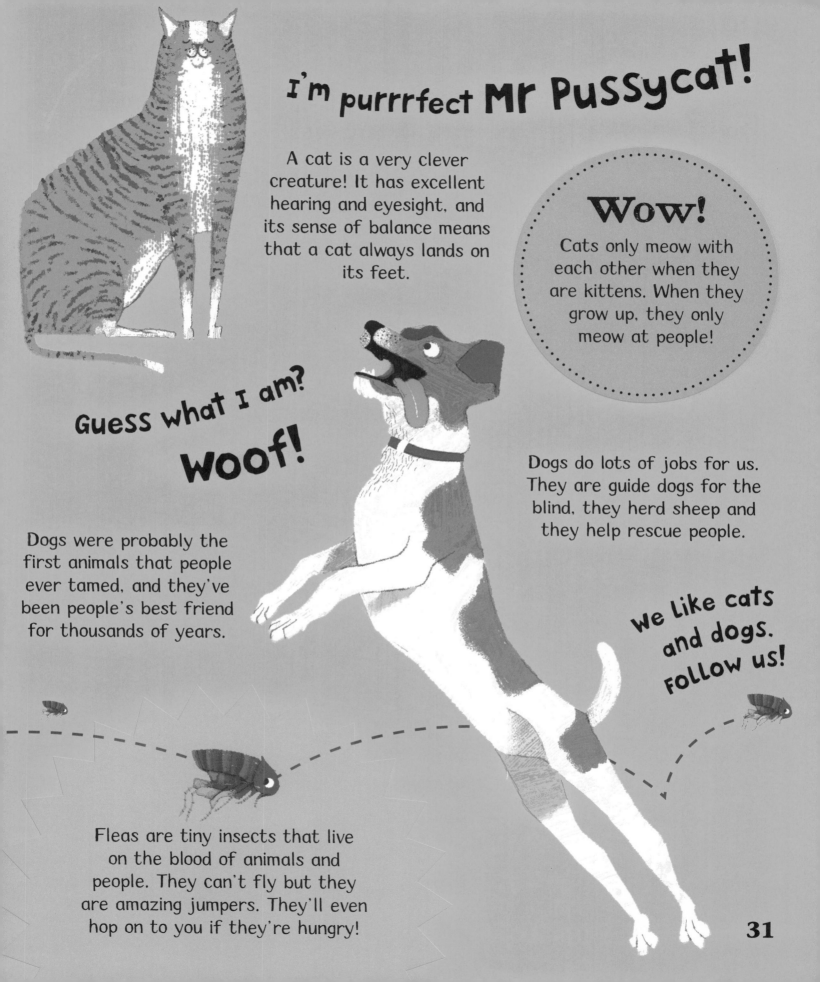

# I'm purrrfect Mr Pussycat!

A cat is a very clever creature! It has excellent hearing and eyesight, and its sense of balance means that a cat always lands on its feet.

## Wow!
Cats only meow with each other when they are kittens. When they grow up, they only meow at people!

### Guess what I am? WOOf!

Dogs were probably the first animals that people ever tamed, and they've been people's best friend for thousands of years.

Dogs do lots of jobs for us. They are guide dogs for the blind, they herd sheep and they help rescue people.

### We like cats and dogs. FOLLOW us!

Fleas are tiny insects that live on the blood of animals and people. They can't fly but they are amazing jumpers. They'll even hop on to you if they're hungry!

# Smelly business

There is something that all animals, large or small, have in common. Do you know what it is? They poo!

My poo looks like pepper!

I'm a civet and I like coffee!

An elephant makes 50 kilograms of poo every day. That's roughly the same weight as a 12-year-old boy! Elephant poo can be turned into paper.

His poo doesn't smell.

Civets look a bit like cats. In parts of Asia and Africa, where coffee plants grow, civets eat coffee and then poop out the bean. Farmers use the stinky bean to make very expensive coffee. YUCKY!

Dung beetles roll animal dung into big balls, bury it and then snack on it later!

Hello, dung beetles!

## Wow!

The horned dung beetle is the world's strongest insect. And its favourite food is dung!